WELCOME TO THE U.S.A.

WASHINGTON

Written by Ann Heinrichs   Illustrated by Matt Kania
Content Adviser: Garry Schalliol, Director of Heritage Resource
Center and Outreach Services Division, Washington State
Historical Society, Olympia, Washington

The Child's World

Published in the United States of America by The Child's World®
PO Box 326 • Chanhassen, MN 55317-0326
800-599-READ • www.childsworld.com

Photo Credits

Cover: Photodisc; frontispiece: Brand X Pictures.

Interior: AP/Wide World Photo/Cheryl Hatch: 29; Corbis: 13 (Richard A. Cooke), 17 (Richard Cummins), 18 (Connie Ricca), 25 (Josef Scaylea), 30 (Gunter Marx Photography); Friends of Washoe: 34; Getty Images: 22 (Aurora/Peter Essick), 26 (Ron Wurzer); Michael T. Sedam/Corbis: 14, 21; Washington State Tourism: 6 (Lewis County Convention & Visitors Burea/Loren Lane), 10 (Deana Edmiston), 33 (Jim Poth); Wenatchee World: 9.

Acknowledgments

The Child's World®: Mary Berendes, Publishing Director

Editorial Directions, Inc.: E. Russell Primm, Editorial Director; Katie Marsico, Associate Editor; Judith Shiffer, Assistant Editor; Matt Messbarger, Editorial Assistant; Susan Hindman, Copy Editor; Melissa McDaniel, Proofreader; Kevin Cunningham, Peter Garnham, Matt Messbarger, Olivia Nellums, Chris Simms, Molly Symmonds, Katherine Trickle, Carl Stephen Wender, Fact Checkers; Tim Griffin/IndexServ, Indexer; Cian Loughlin O'Day, Photo Researcher and Editor

The Design Lab: Kathleen Petelinsek, Design and Art Production

Library of Congress Cataloging-in-Publication Data
Heinrichs, Ann.
  Washington / by Ann Heinrichs.
    p. cm — (Welcome to the U.S.A.)
  Includes bibliographical references and index.
  ISBN 1-59296-489-3 (library bound : alk. paper)
  1. Washington (State)—Juvenile literature. I. Title.
  F891.3.H45 2005
  979.7—dc22   2005013657

Ann Heinrichs is the author of more than 100 books for children and young adults. She has also enjoyed successful careers as a children's book editor and an advertising copywriter. Ann grew up in Fort Smith, Arkansas, and lives in Chicago, Illinois.

About the Author
Ann Heinrichs

Matt Kania loves maps and, as a kid, dreamed of making them. In school he studied geography and cartography, and today he makes maps for a living. Matt's favorite thing about drawing maps is learning about the places they represent. Many of the maps he has created can be found in books, magazines, videos, Web sites, and public places.

About the
Map Illustrator
Matt Kania

On the cover: Look up! Check out the Space Needle in Seattle.
On page one: Scenic Mount Rainier towers above Washington's wilderness.

OUR WASHINGTON TRIP

Washington's Nickname:
The Evergreen State

WELCOME TO WASHINGTON

Hey—it's time for a trip through Washington! You'll have some great adventures there.

You'll climb mountains and hike through forests. You'll eat salmon roasted on a stick. You'll try out the latest computer games. You'll sail through the sky over a city. You'll watch gigantic whales leaping in the ocean. You'll eat all the apple pies you can hold. And you'll meet some frisky chimpanzees!

That's a lot of activity, so don't wait. Just follow that loopy dotted line. Or else skip around. Either way, you're in for lots of fun. Now, buckle up and let's hit the road!

Washington was named after the 1st president, George Washington. It's the only state named after a president.

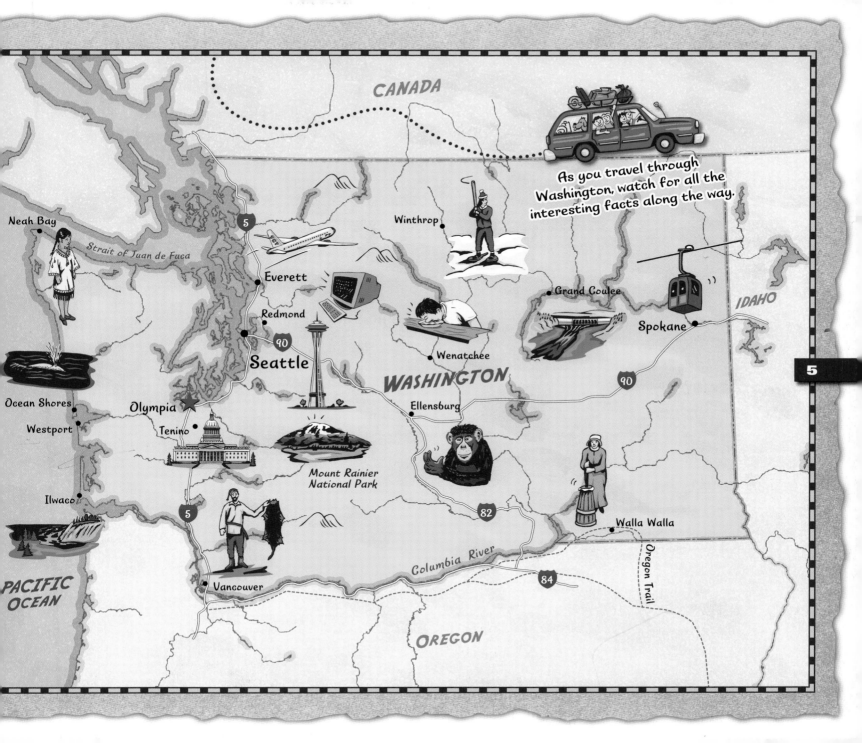

CANADA

As you travel through Washington, watch for all the interesting facts along the way.

Neah Bay

Strait of Juan de Fuca

Winthrop

5

Everett

Grand Coulee

IDAHO

Redmond

Spokane

90

Seattle

Wenatchee

5

WASHINGTON

Ocean Shores

Olympia

Ellensburg

90

Westport

Tenino

Mount Rainier National Park

Ilwaco

82

Walla Walla

Vancouver

Columbia River

84

Oregon Trail

PACIFIC OCEAN

OREGON

Mount Rainier is Washington's tallest mountain. Do you think you could hike to the top?

Mount Saint Helens is a volcano in the Cascade Range. It erupted in 1980.

Mount Rainier National Park

Hike along the mountain's edge. Or try climbing toward the peak. Maybe you'd like camping along a mountain stream. Or just lounging in a meadow of wildflowers. You're enjoying Mount Rainier National Park!

Snow-covered Mount Rainier is Washington's highest peak. It's part of the Cascade Mountain Range. The Cascades run through Washington from north to south.

The Columbia River flows through eastern Washington. It also forms most of the state's southern border. Much of eastern Washington is very dry. The west coast faces the Pacific Ocean. The Olympic **Peninsula** juts out in the northwest. Puget Sound separates it from the mainland to the east.

The Olympic Mountains rise on the Olympic Peninsula.

Highest Temperature: Grant County July 24, 1928 Ice Harbor Dam August 5, 1961 118°F (48°C)

Lowest Temperature: Mazama and Winthrop December 30, 1968 -48°F (-44°C)

CANADA

IDAHO

Mazama • • Winthrop

Olympic Peninsula

Olympic Mountains

• Seattle

Puget Sound

Forget climbing to the top! About 10,000 people try every year. Only about half of them make it. It's too steep for me!

Grant County

Mount Rainier National Park

Mount Rainier

Longmire • • Paradise

Tacoma is a Native American name for Mount Rainier.

Puget Sound is a waterway full of islands, inlets, and bays. The large port city of Seattle faces the sound.

PACIFIC OCEAN

Mount Saint Helens

Cascade Range

Ice Harbor Dam

OREGON

Colombia River

HIGHEST AND LOWEST POINTS
Highest: Mount Rainier at 14,410 feet (4,392 m)
Lowest: Sea level along the Pacific Ocean

Mount Rainier is a volcano. But it hasn't erupted for more than 100 years.

Longmire and Paradise are popular destinations in Mount Rainier National Park.

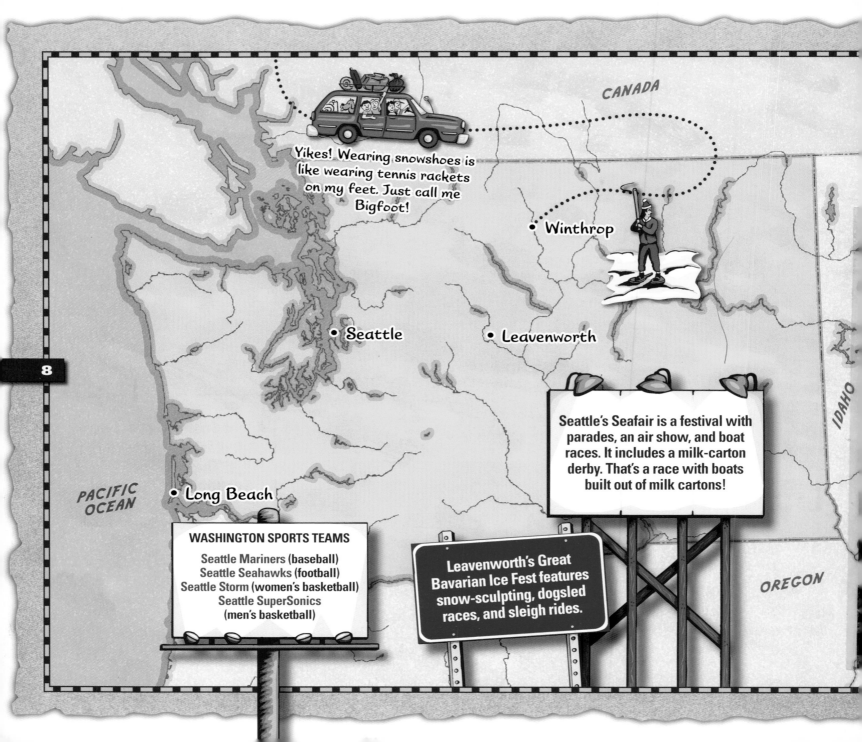

8

Yikes! Wearing snowshoes is like wearing tennis rackets on my feet. Just call me Bigfoot!

• Winthrop

• Seattle

• Leavenworth

PACIFIC OCEAN

• Long Beach

CANADA

IDAHO

OREGON

Seattle's Seafair is a festival with parades, an air show, and boat races. It includes a milk-carton derby. That's a race with boats built out of milk cartons!

WASHINGTON SPORTS TEAMS

Seattle Mariners (baseball)
Seattle Seahawks (football)
Seattle Storm (women's basketball)
Seattle SuperSonics
(men's basketball)

Leavenworth's Great Bavarian Ice Fest features snow-sculpting, dogsled races, and sleigh rides.

Winthrop's Snowshoe Softball Tournament

How fast can you run? Try putting on some big old snowshoes. Then try running in the snow. You wouldn't be so fast, would you?

That's what people do in Winthrop. They hold the Snowshoe Softball Tournament every winter. Everyone runs the bases wearing snowshoes!

People in Washington have lots of winter fun. They ski on the snowy mountain slopes. Or they go ice-skating and snowmobiling. When it's warmer, they go hiking or boating. Mountain climbing is popular, too. Do you love the outdoors? Then Washington's the place for you!

Home run! Run as fast as your snowshoes will carry you!

Kite flyers from around the world come to the International Kite Festival in Long Beach.

The Cascades' western slopes have thick forests. The eastern slopes are steeper and rockier.

Watching the Gray Whales

These deer call a Washington forest home.

More than 20,000 gray whales migrate past Washington between March and May.

You probably know that birds **migrate.** But did you know that whales migrate, too? Gray whales have their babies near Baja California. Then they migrate north to the Arctic Ocean. Want to watch them? Just go to Westport or Ocean Shores!

Washington is home to many wild animals. Deer and elk live in the forested mountains. Mountain goats scamper on the rocky slopes. Overhead, you'll see graceful eagles and hawks. Ducks, herons, and other waterbirds inhabit the wetlands. The Rocky Mountains reach into northeastern Washington. There you'll find moose and even grizzly bears.

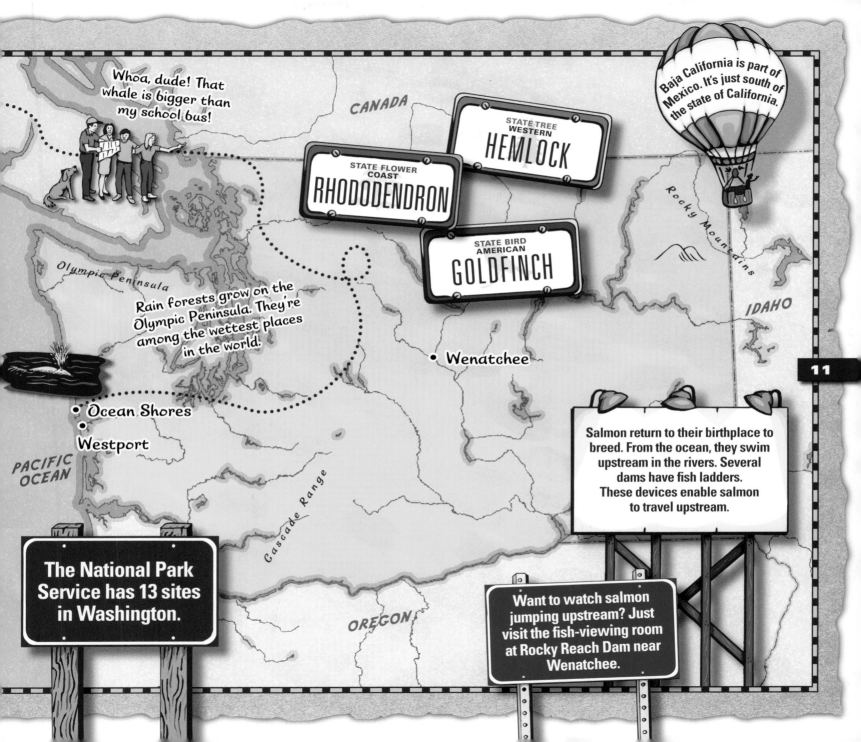

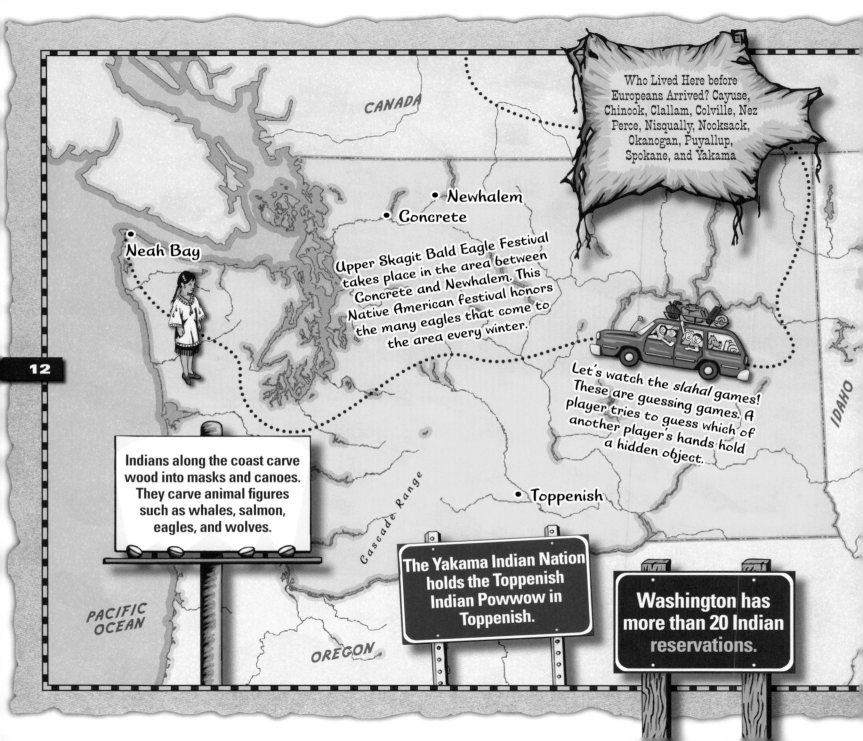

CANADA

Who Lived Here before Europeans Arrived? Cayuse, Chinook, Clallam, Colville, Nez Perce, Nisqually, Nooksack, Okanogan, Puyallup, Spokane, and Yakama

• Newhalem

• Concrete

Neah Bay

Upper Skagit Bald Eagle Festival takes place in the area between Concrete and Newhalem. This Native American festival honors the many eagles that come to the area every winter.

Let's watch the slahal games! These are guessing games. A player tries to guess which of another player's hands hold a hidden object.

IDAHO

Indians along the coast carve wood into masks and canoes. They carve animal figures such as whales, salmon, eagles, and wolves.

Cascade Range

• Toppenish

The Yakama Indian Nation holds the Toppenish Indian Powwow in Toppenish.

Washington has more than 20 Indian reservations.

PACIFIC OCEAN

OREGON

Makah Days in Neah Bay

Ever been in a longhouse? Learn about Indian culture at Makah Days.

Salmon is roasting on sticks around the fire. Eager paddlers take off for the canoe races. Soon the dances and fireworks will begin. You're attending Makah Days!

The Makah are one of Washington's Native American tribes. **Traditionally,** they made their living from the sea. They caught salmon, seals, and whales. Even children had small canoes for practice. Makah homes were longhouses built of cedar. Each one housed children, parents, and grandparents.

Several Indian tribes lived near Washington's coast. They caught salmon and gathered clams. Other groups lived east of the Cascades. They hunted, fished, and gathered wild plants.

13

14

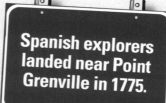

Want a great view of the Pacific Ocean?
Head to Cape Disappointment!

Spanish explorers landed near Point Grenville in 1775.

Cape Disappointment State Park

Traders wanted Washington's valuable fur-bearing animals. They had heard of a great river here, too. It emptied into the Pacific Ocean.

English fur trader John Meares sailed by in 1788. But he found no river. So he named a rocky point Cape Disappointment. U.S. fur trader Robert Gray was luckier. He found the river in 1792. He named it the Columbia River. Then the United States claimed the region.

Explorers Meriwether Lewis and William Clark traveled cross-country. Following the Columbia River, they arrived at Cape Disappointment. But they were not disappointed. They reached the Pacific Ocean in 1805. Just visit Cape Disappointment. You'll learn all about their trip!

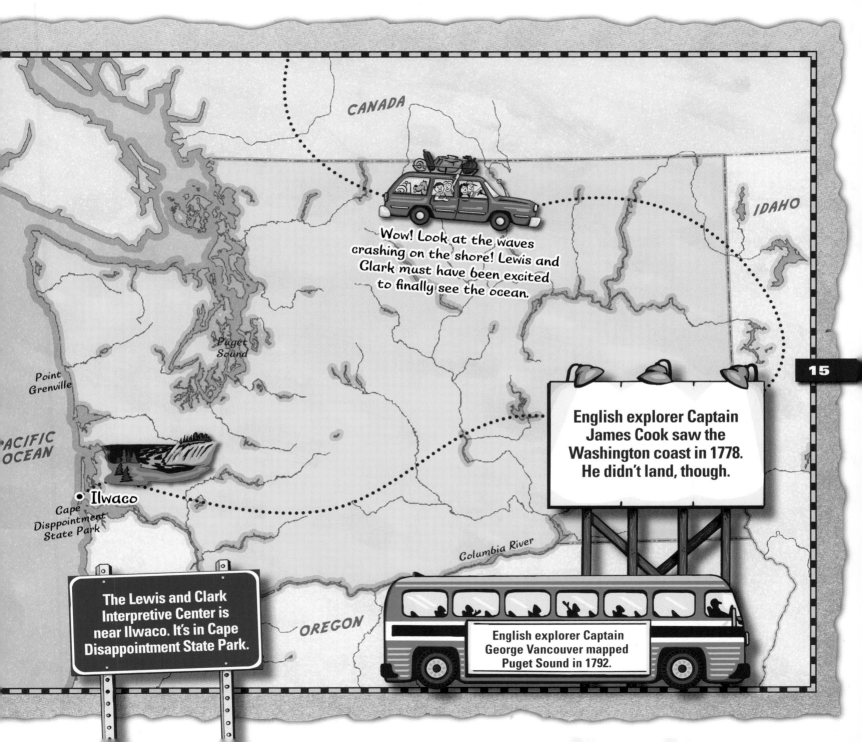

CANADA

IDAHO

Wow! Look at the waves crashing on the shore! Lewis and Clark must have been excited to finally see the ocean.

Puget Sound

Point Grenville

English explorer Captain James Cook saw the Washington coast in 1778. He didn't land, though.

PACIFIC OCEAN

• Ilwaco

Cape Disppointment State Park

Columbia River

The Lewis and Clark Interpretive Center is near Ilwaco. It's in Cape Disappointment State Park.

OREGON

English explorer Captain George Vancouver mapped Puget Sound in 1792.

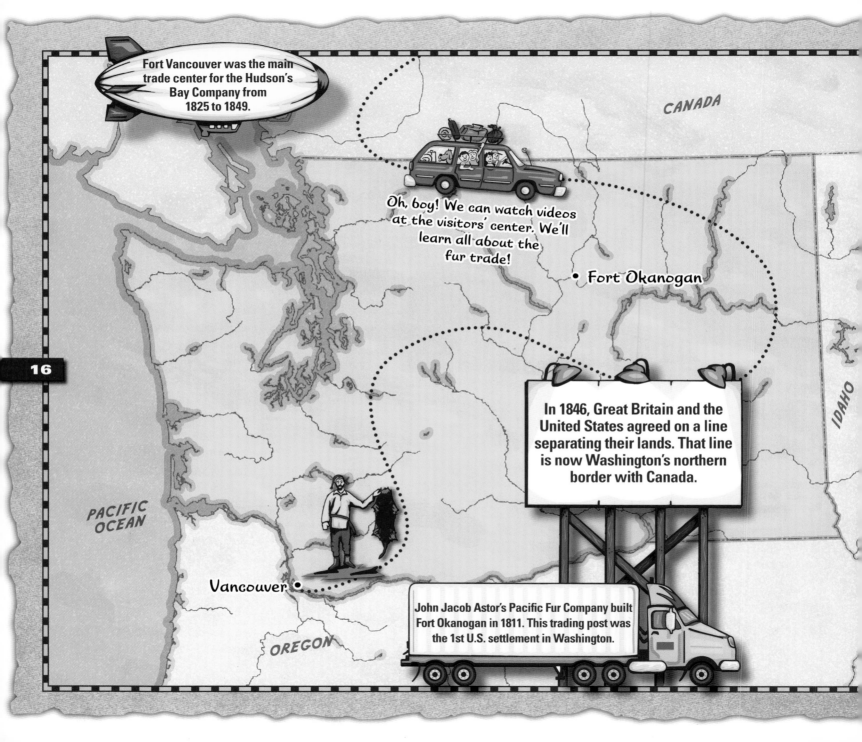

Smell delicious food cooked on wood-burning stoves. Hear the carpenter hammering away. Watch the blacksmith pounding metal into tools. You're at Fort Vancouver! It used to be a fur-trading post. You can watch its old-time activities every summer.

Fur traders had many trading posts in Washington. People from the United States and Great Britain built them. Both nations were trying to control the region.

A British company built Fort Vancouver in 1825. Hundreds of people worked there. Many were trappers who ventured into the wilderness. Others worked in the nearby village. They grew crops and built ships. They supplied whatever the fort needed.

17

Would you have made a good fur trader? Visit Fort Vancouver and find out!

Washington was the 42nd state to enter the Union. It joined on November 11, 1889.

Whitman Mission near Walla Walla

Pioneers stopped and rested at Whitman Mission. They traveled west in covered wagons.

Try churning some butter. It's hard work! Then try making some adobe bricks. You make them with clay and straw. You're enjoying a summer weekend at Whitman **Mission**!

Marcus and Narcissa Whitman once lived here. They opened a mission for Cayuse Indians in 1836. Many **pioneers** stopped by, too. They were following the Oregon Trail. They had traveled far in covered wagons. They hoped to build farms in the West.

The Whitmans and the pioneers had many skills. They made all they needed by hand. Here you can try out those skills yourself!

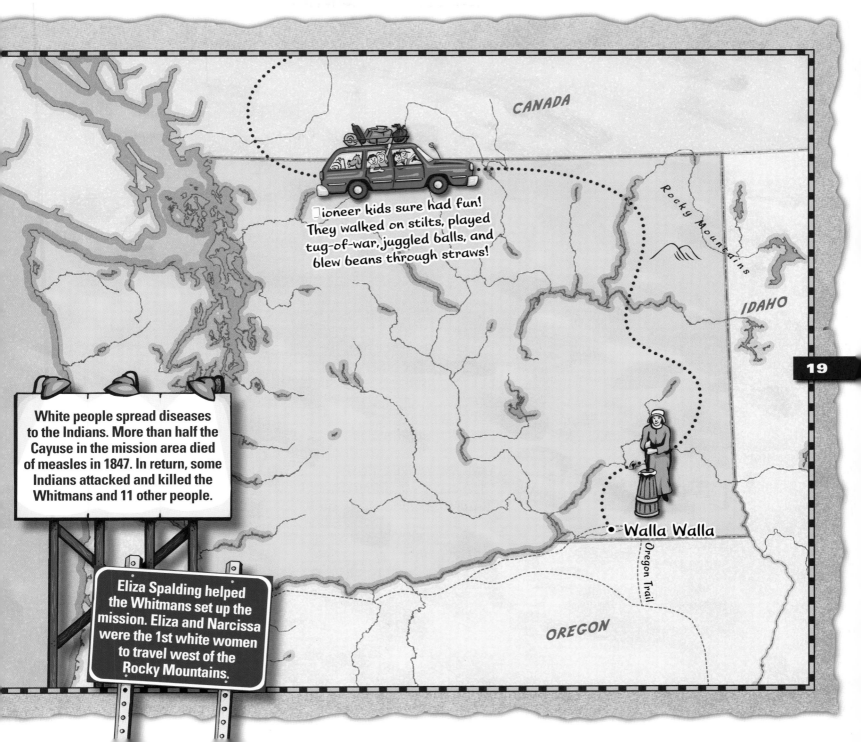

Pioneer kids sure had fun! They walked on stilts, played tug-of-war, juggled balls, and blew beans through straws!

CANADA

Rocky Mountains

IDAHO

19

White people spread diseases to the Indians. More than half the Cayuse in the mission area died of measles in 1847. In return, some Indians attacked and killed the Whitmans and 11 other people.

Eliza Spalding helped the Whitmans set up the mission. Eliza and Narcissa were the 1st white women to travel west of the Rocky Mountains.

Walla Walla

Oregon Trail

OREGON

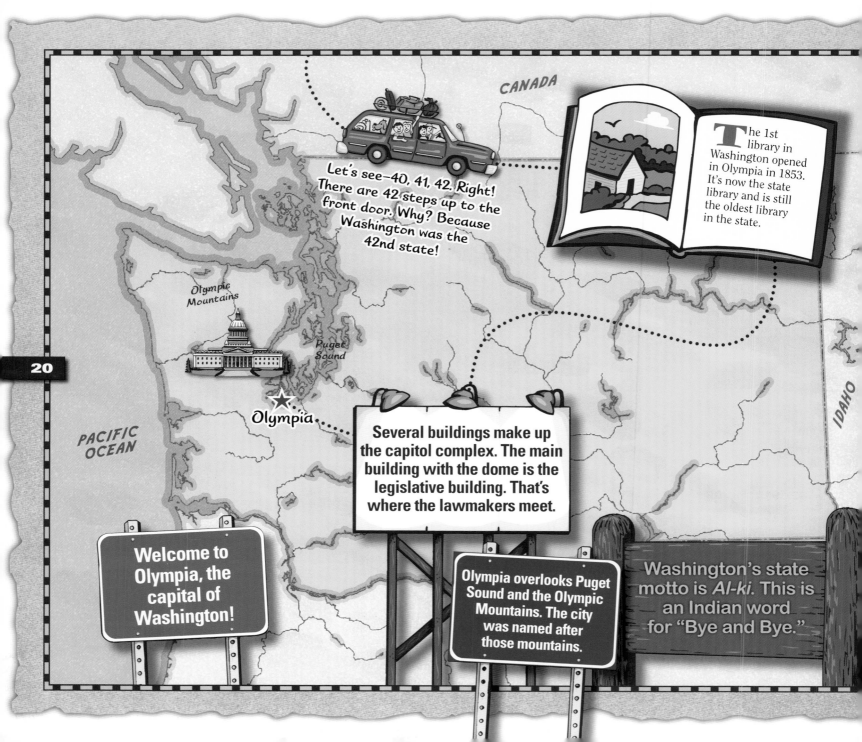

CANADA

Let's see—40, 41, 42. Right! There are 42 steps up to the front door. Why? Because Washington was the 42nd state!

The 1st library in Washington opened in Olympia in 1853. It's now the state library and is still the oldest library in the state.

Olympic Mountains

Puget Sound

PACIFIC OCEAN

★ Olympia

IDAHO

Several buildings make up the capitol complex. The main building with the dome is the legislative building. That's where the lawmakers meet.

Welcome to Olympia, the capital of Washington!

Olympia overlooks Puget Sound and the Olympic Mountains. The city was named after those mountains.

Washington's state motto is *Al-ki*. This is an Indian word for "Bye and Bye."

The State Capitol in Olympia

Washington's capitol is a **symbol** of strength. It's also just plain strong! An earthquake struck in 2001. The dome cracked, and ten columns moved. Today, the restored building stands strong and proud.

The capitol is the center of state government. Washington has three branches of government. One branch makes the state laws. Its members meet in the capitol. The governor heads another branch. Its job is to carry out the laws. Judges make up the third branch. They listen to cases in courts. Then they decide whether laws have been broken.

Look up! You're staring at the dome atop Washington's capitol.

The earthquake of February 28, 2001, registered 6.8 on the Richter scale. That's the measure of an earthquake's energy.

Want to see an awesome light show? Just head to the Grand Coulee Dam!

22

Get into the glass-walled elevator. Then ride right down the face of the dam. At the bottom, there's a massive power plant. It creates electricity for homes miles away. But the best part comes after dark. You'll watch a spectacular light show. It dances across the wall of the dam!

You're exploring the Grand Coulee Dam. Washington workers began building large dams in the 1930s. The dams do a lot for the state. They direct water into farmers' fields. They also control floods and produce electric power.

Construction began on Grand Coulee Dam in 1934. It was completed in 1942.

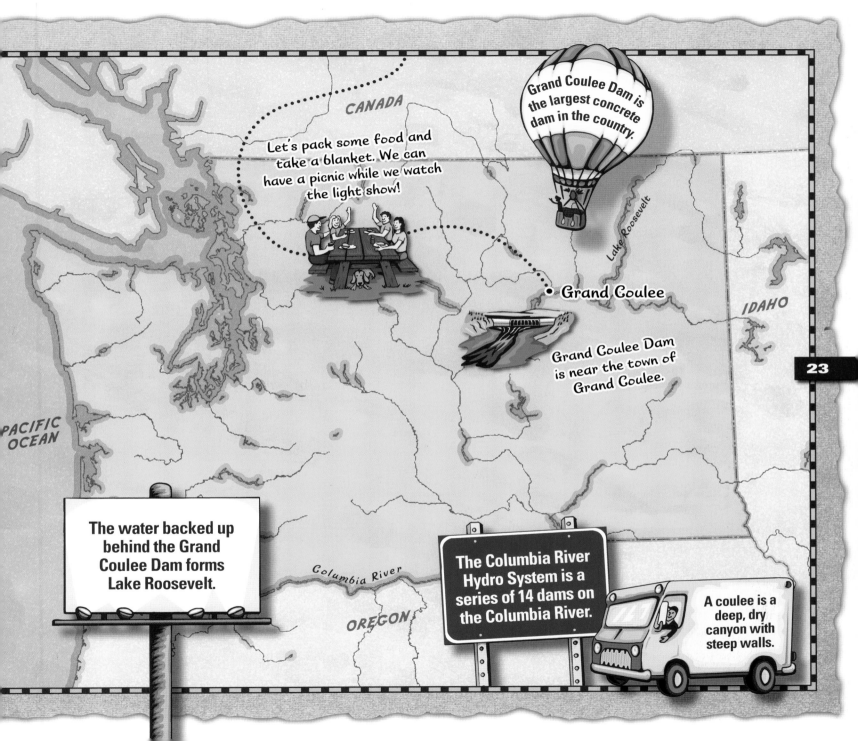

CANADA

Let's pack some food and take a blanket. We can have a picnic while we watch the light show!

Grand Coulee Dam is the largest concrete dam in the country.

Lake Roosevelt

• Grand Coulee

Grand Coulee Dam is near the town of Grand Coulee.

IDAHO

PACIFIC OCEAN

The water backed up behind the Grand Coulee Dam forms Lake Roosevelt.

Columbia River

The Columbia River Hydro System is a series of 14 dams on the Columbia River.

OREGON

A coulee is a deep, dry canyon with steep walls.

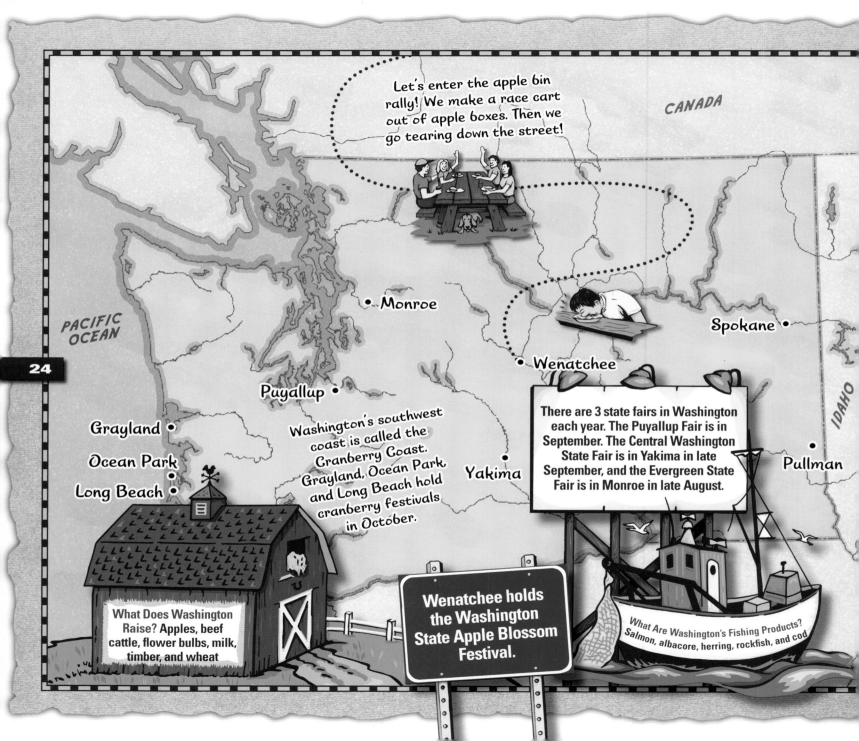

Wenatchee's Apple Harvest Festival

The Green Bluff Apple Festival is held in Spokane.

Do you like apple pie? How many apple pies can you eat? You'll find out at the Washington Apple Harvest Festival. Just enter its pie-eating contest!

This festival celebrates Washington's favorite fruit. No other state grows more apples than Washington. And no state grows more pears, either. Wheat is the top crop, though. A lot of it grows in eastern Washington.

Much of eastern Washington is naturally dry. But farms in its river valleys are very fertile. That's because **irrigation** brings water to the fields. Many farmers raise cattle for beef and milk. Trees are valuable products, too.

Are apples your favorite fruit? Then Washington's the state for you!

25

Pullman holds the National Lentil Festival. Lentils are legumes, just as peas are. A lentil is shaped like a squashed pea.

Are you a computer whiz? Test your skills at the Microsoft Visitor Center!

Bill Gates and Paul Allen founded Microsoft in 1975.

The Microsoft Visitor Center in Redmond

Make a movie and star in it, too. Try your luck at the latest computer games. See the first personal computer ever made. Discover what the future holds for computers. You're exploring the Microsoft Visitor Center!

Microsoft is one of Washington's biggest companies. It sells its products all over the world.

Washington was busy during World War II (1939–1945). It made military aircraft and ships. Its farms also supplied food for the troops.

Many new **industries** grew after the war. One is the Boeing aircraft company. Another is Weyerhaeuser Paper. And, of course, there's Microsoft!

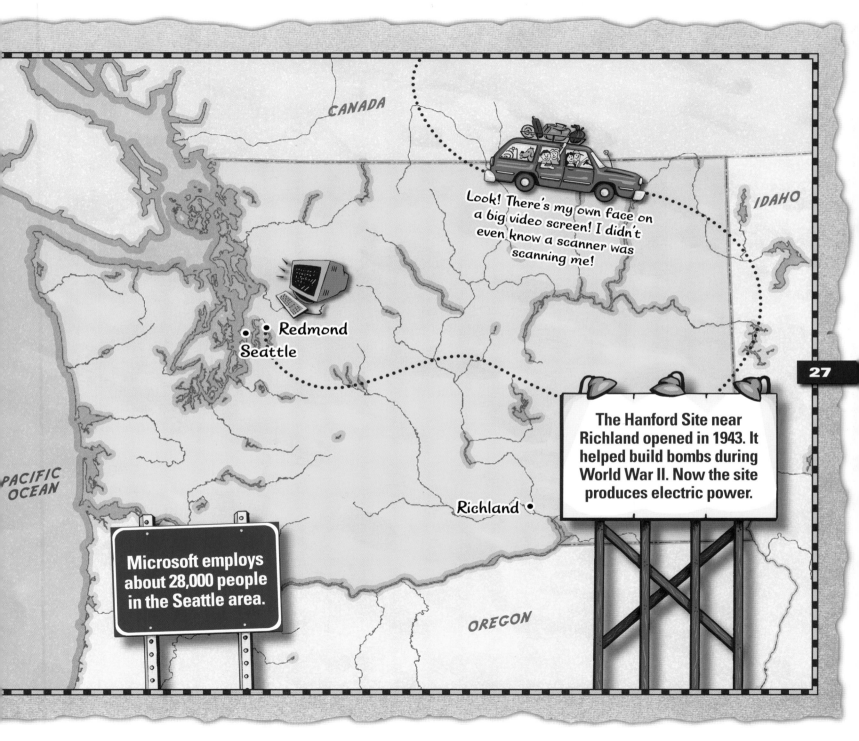

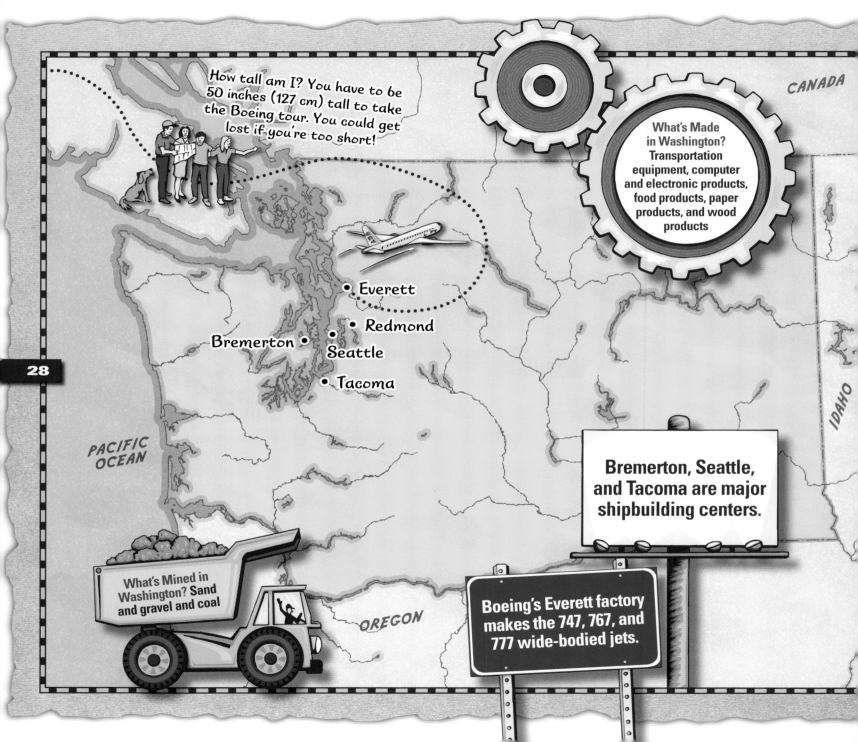

How tall am I? You have to be 50 inches (127 cm) tall to take the Boeing tour. You could get lost if you're too short!

CANADA

What's Made in Washington? Transportation equipment, computer and electronic products, food products, paper products, and wood products

• Everett

• Redmond

Bremerton • •
Seattle

• Tacoma

28

PACIFIC OCEAN

IDAHO

Bremerton, Seattle, and Tacoma are major shipbuilding centers.

What's Mined in Washington? Sand and gravel and coal

OREGON

Boeing's Everett factory makes the 747, 767, and 777 wide-bodied jets.

Everett's Boeing Factory

Have you ever built a model airplane? Your project probably covered a desk or table. Now imagine building a full-size airplane. You need lots of room for that. Just visit the Boeing factory in Everett. No building in the world takes up more space! There you'll see massive airplane parts. And you'll learn how they're put together.

Boeing is the world's largest aircraft maker. Naturally, transportation equipment is Washington's top factory product. Shipbuilding is another big industry. Computer products are also important. Thousands of people work at Microsoft in Redmond. Washington produces many foods and wood products, too.

Ever wonder how planes are made? Tour the Boeing factory in Everett to find out.

People from Asian countries are Washington's largest nonwhite ethnic group.

Seattle's Space Needle lights up over the city.

More than half of Washington's residents live in the Puget Sound Region.

Exploring Seattle

S eattle is a great place to explore. Its tall, pointy Space Needle towers over the city. From the top, you can see for miles. Nearby is the Pacific Science Center. You'll see life-size moving dinosaurs there. Things are moving at the Seattle Aquarium, too. They include otters and octopuses!

Many **immigrants** settled in Seattle. It became Washington's biggest city. It's a major shipping center for Asian trade.

Check out Seattle's Northwest Folklife Festival. You'll eat Greek, Thai, and African foods there. You'll hear the music of Mexico, Scotland, and Japan. And you'll see dances from many Asian lands. All these **ethnic** groups made Washington their home.

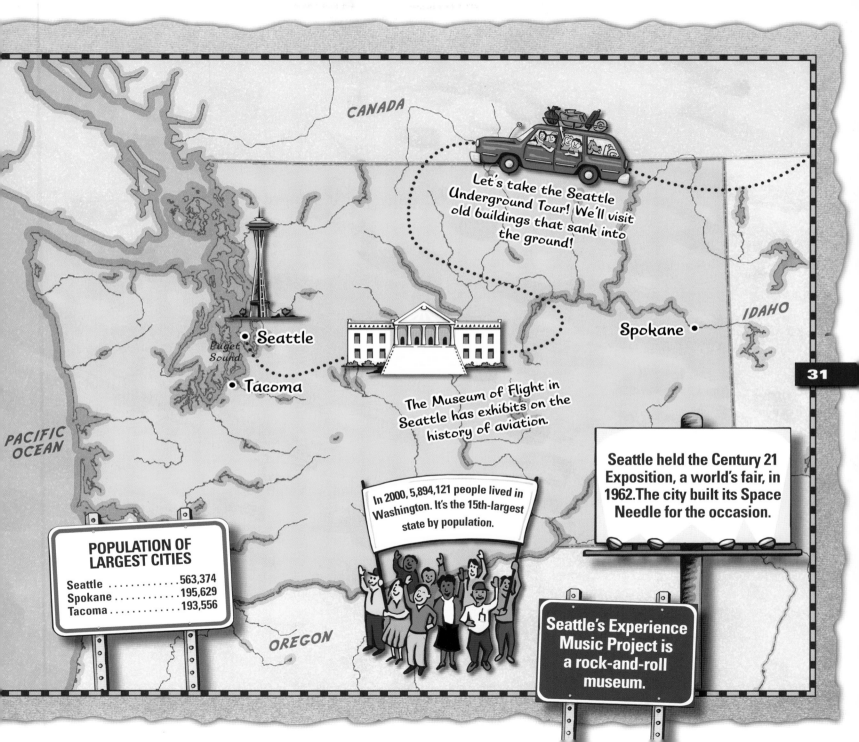

Let's take the Seattle Underground Tour! We'll visit old buildings that sank into the ground!

The Museum of Flight in Seattle has exhibits on the history of aviation.

In 2000, 5,894,121 people lived in Washington. It's the 15th-largest state by population.

Seattle held the Century 21 Exposition, a world's fair, in 1962. The city built its Space Needle for the occasion.

Seattle's Experience Music Project is a rock-and-roll museum.

POPULATION OF LARGEST CITIES

Seattle 563,374
Spokane 195,629
Tacoma 193,556

CANADA

PACIFIC OCEAN

Puget Sound

Seattle

Tacoma

Spokane

IDAHO

OREGON

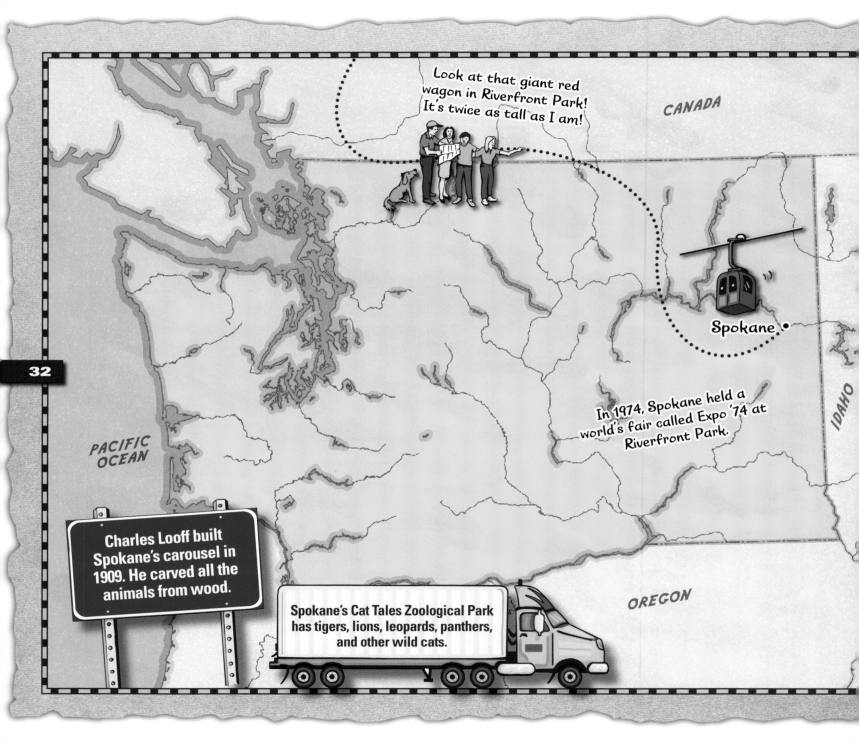

Spokane is a fun place to visit. It has some unusual rides. One is the **carousel** in Riverfront Park. It has fifty-four beautifully decorated horses. Their tails are made from real horse hair. There's a giraffe and a tiger, too. Or maybe you'd prefer the Chinese dragon chairs!

Are you tired of riding in circles? Then take the Gondola SkyRide. It moves along wires high in the sky. You get on the gondola in Riverfront Park. Then you go soaring high above the city. Look down and see the thundering Spokane Falls. Whee!

Ready to relax after that carousel ride? Enjoy a stroll through scenic Riverfront Park.

The Chimps of Ellensburg

Can chimpanzees tell you things? They sure can! Just attend a Chimposium. They're held at Central Washington University in Ellensburg. You'll meet several frisky chimps there. And they're experts at sign language!

These chimps use sign language to chat with humans. They also use it to talk with each other. They sometimes even make signs while they sleep. They're dreaming!

Scientists at Ellensburg are studying how chimpanzees communicate. They watch how the chimps get along. The chimps play and even work on projects together. Would you like to study chimps someday?

What do chimpanzees like to talk about? Find out at Central Washington University.

Chimpanzees can live to be more than 50 years old.

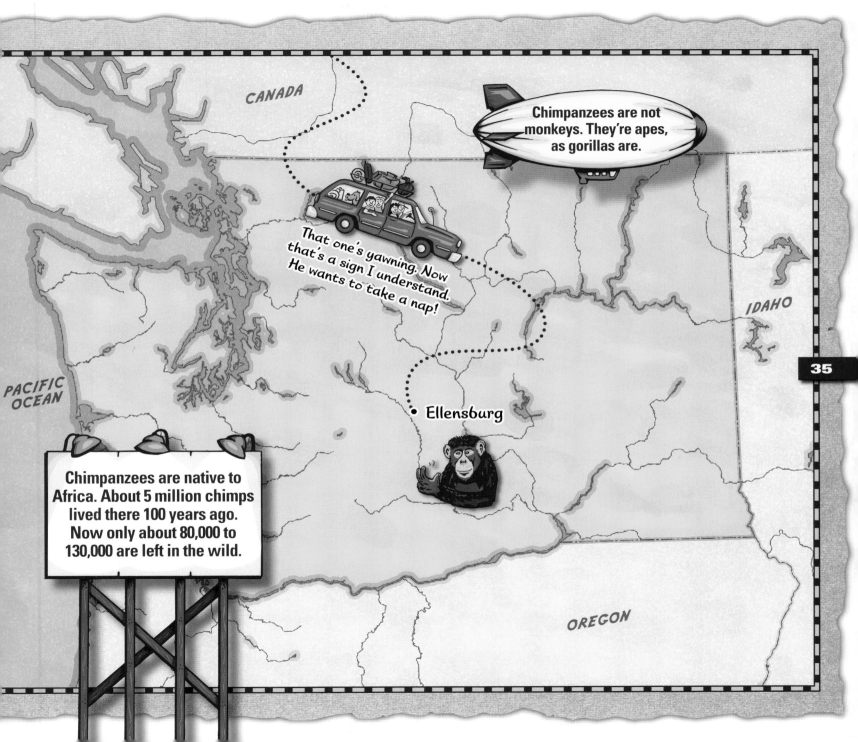

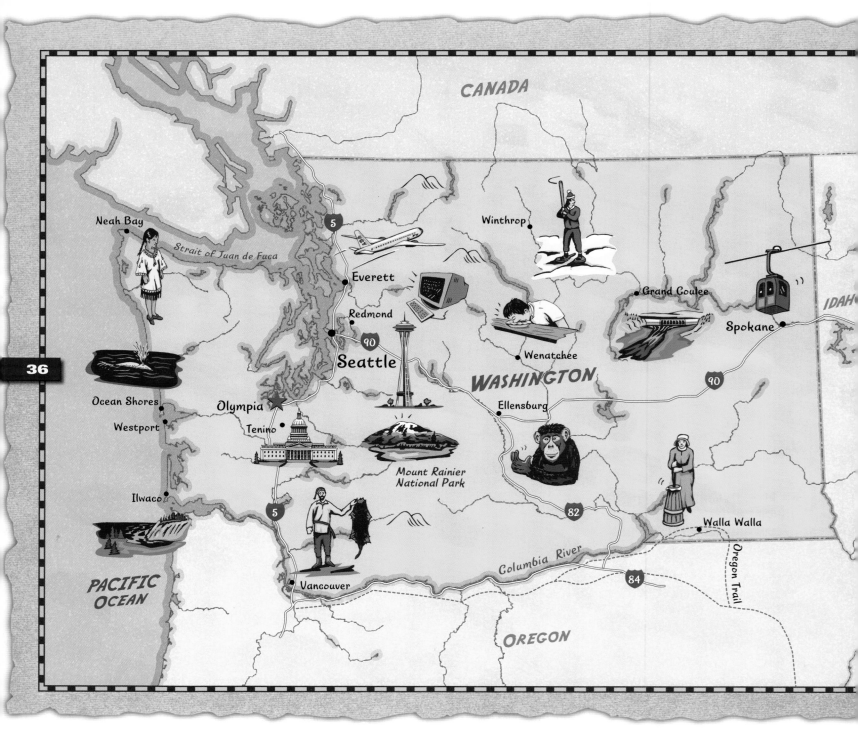

OUR TRIP

We visited many amazing places on our trip! We also met a lot of interesting people along the way. Look at the map on the left. Use your finger to trace all the places we have been.

Who was Washington named after? See page 4 for the answer.

What is Mount Saint Helens? Page 6 has the answer.

How many gray whales migrate past Washington in the spring? See page 10 for the answer.

When was Fort Okanogan built? Look on page 16 for the answer.

Why does the capitol have 42 steps? Page 20 has the answer.

What is a coulee? Turn to page 23 for the answer.

How many dams make up the Columbia River Hydro System? Look on page 23 for the answer.

How many Microsoft employees live in the Seattle area? Turn to page 27 for the answer.

That was a great trip! We have traveled all over Washington.

There are a few places that we didn't have time for, though. Next time, we plan to visit Wolf Haven in Tenino. Visitors can view wolves, foxes, and coyotes. They learn how wolves live in the wild and why it's important to protect them.

More Places to Visit in Washington

WORDS TO KNOW

carousel (kar-uh-SELL) a merry-go-round

ethnic (ETH-nik) relating to a person's race or nationality

immigrants (IM-uh-gruhnts) people who move to another country

industries (IN-duh-streez) types of business

irrigation (ihr-uh-GAY-shuhn) a method of bringing water to fields through ditches or pipes

migrate (MY-grate) to move from location to location, often following the seasons

mission (MISH-uhn) a place where people try to spread their religion

peninsula (puh-NIN-soo-lah) a piece of land almost completely surrounded by water

pioneers (pye-uh-NEERZ) people who move into an unsettled area

reservations (rez-ur-VAY-shunz) land set aside for use by American Indians

symbol (SIMM-bull) something that stands for an idea or value

traditionally (truh-DISH-uh-nul-lee) following long-held customs

Washington covers 66,544 square miles (172,348 sq km). It's the 20th-largest state in size.

STATE SYMBOLS

State bird: American goldfinch (wild canary)

State dance: Square dance

State fish: Steelhead trout

State flower: Coast rhododendron

State folk song: "Roll On, Columbia, Roll On"

State fossil: Columbian mammoth

State fruit: Apple

State gem: Petrified wood

State grass: Bluebunch wheatgrass

State insect: Green darner dragonfly

State ship: *President Washington*

State tree: Western hemlock

State flag

State seal

STATE SONG

"Washington, My Home"
Words and music by Helen Davis

This is my country; God gave it to me;
I will protect it, ever keep it free.
Small towns and cities rest here in the sun,
Filled with our laughter, "Thy will be done."

Washington, my home;
Where ever I may roam;
This is my land, my native land,
Washington, my home.
Our verdant forest green,
Caressed by silv'ry stream.
From mountain peak to fields of wheat,
Washington, my home.

There's peace you feel and understand
In this, our own beloved land.
We greet the day with head held high,
And forward ever is our cry.
We'll happy ever be
As people always free.
For you and me a destiny;
Washington my home.

FAMOUS PEOPLE

Boeing, William (1881–1956), aircraft manufacturer

Carlson, Chester F. (1906–1968), inventor

Chihuly, Dale (1941–), artist

Crosby, Bing (1903–1977), singer and actor

Crutcher, Chris (1946–), children's author

Cunningham, Merce (1919–), choreographer

Gates, Bill (1955–), billionaire who helped create Microsoft

Guterson, David (1956–), novelist

Herbert, Frank (1920–1986), novelist

Jones, Chuck (1912–2002), animator who helped create the *Bugs Bunny* cartoons

Jones, Quincy (1933–), composer, bandleader

Kehret, Peg (1936–), children's author

Kenny G (1956–), musician

Larson, Gary (1950–), cartoonist who created *The Far Side*

Ohno, Apolo Anton (1982–), speed skater and Olympic medalist

Rashad, Ahmad (1949–), sportscaster

Sandberg, Ryne (1959–), baseball player

Scobee, Francis (1939–1986), astronaut

Seattle (1786–1866), American Indian chief

Smohalla (1820–1895), American Indian and religious leader

West, Adam (1928–), actor

Wilson, August (1945–), playwright

TO FIND OUT MORE

At the Library
Brown, Jonatha A. *Bill Gates.* Milwaukee: Weekly Reader Early Learning Library, 2004.

Cone, Molly, and Sidnee Wheelwright (photographer). *Come Back, Salmon: How a Group of Dedicated Kids Adopted Pigeon Creek and Brought It Back to Life.* San Francisco: Sierra Club Books for Children, 1992.

Furgang, Kathy. *Mt. St. Helens: The Smoking Mountain.* New York: PowerKids, 2001.

Ryan, Marla Felkins, and Linda Schmittroth, (editors). *Chinook.* San Diego: Blackbirch Press, 2004.

Seattle, Chief, and Susan Jeffers (illustrator). *Brother Eagle, Sister Sky: A Message from Chief Seattle.* New York: Dial Books, 1991.

On the Web
Visit our home page for lots of links about Washington: *http://www.childsworld.com/links*

Note to Parents, Teachers, and Librarians: We routinely verify our Web links to make sure they are safe, active sites—so encourage your readers to check them out!

Places to Visit or Contact
Washington State Historical Museum
1911 Pacific Avenue
Tacoma, WA 98402
888/238-4373
For more information about the history of Washington

Washington State Tourism
PO Box 42525
Olympia, WA 98504
800/544-1800
For more information about traveling in Washington

INDEX

Bye, Evergreen State.
We had a great time.
We'll come back soon!